The Chester Books of Madrigal
6. SMOKING AND DRINKING
Edited by Anthony G. Petti

For Dean Applegate

SMOKING

			Page
1.	Michael East	*O metaphysical tobacco* SSATB	1
2.	Thomas Weelkes	*Come, Sirrah Jack, ho* SAB	4
3.	Thomas Ravenscroft	*Tobacco fumes away* SATB; solo ad lib.	6
4.	John Wilson	*Ahey for and aho* SATB (antiphonal)	9
5.	Henry Aldrich	*Good, good indeed* (round) 4 voices	14

DRINKING

6.	Anonymous	*Quand je bois* (Tourdion) SATB	15
7.	Arnold von Bruck	*So trinken wir alle* SSATB	16
8.	Pierre Certon	*C'est trop parlé de Bacchus* SATB	19
9.	Francesco Corteccia	*Bacco, Bacco* SATB	23
10.	Juan del Encina	*Hoy comamos y bebamos* SATB; soli ad lib.	24
11.	Henning Dedekind	*Trink ich Wein* SABar.	26
12.	Andrea Gabrieli	*Canto, canto, festa, festa* SMez. AA	27
13.	Orlandus Lassus	*Ein guter Wein* SAATB	28
14.	Juan Ponce	*Ave, color vini* SATB	23
15.	Thomas Ravenscroft	*Give us once a drink* SATB; solo ad lib.	35
16.	Thomas Ravenscroft	*Toss the pot* SATB; solo ad lib.	36
17.	Thomas Ravenscroft	*Trudge away quickly* SATB; solo ad lib.	38
18.	Thomas Ravenscroft (ed.)	Rounds from *Pammelia*:	40
		(i) *Banbury ale* 4 voices	
		(ii) *Donnez à boire* 4 voices	
		(iii) *Now kiss the cup, Cousin* 3 voices	
		(iv) *He that will an alehouse keep* 3 voices	
		(v) *Hey down a down* 3 voices	
		(vi) *Hey ho, nobody at home* 5 voices	
		(vii) *White wine and sugar* 5 voices	
19.	John Hilton	Rounds from *Catch that Catch Can*:	41
		(i) *Call George again, boy* 3 voices	
		(ii) *If you will drink for pleasure* 3 voices	
		(iii) *O ale ab alendo* 3 voices	
		(iv) *O yes, O yes* 3 voices	

Editor's Notes   43

CHESTER MUSIC

Cover:
May (Taurus/Gemini) from the
Très Riches Heures du Duc de Berry.
Reproduced by kind permission of the Musée Condé, Chantilly.

1. O METAPHYSICAL TOBACCO

Michael East (c. 1580 - c. 1647)

CH 55614

2

far as from_____ Mo - roc - co, fetched as far as from Mo-roc - co, fetched as far as

- co, fetched as far as from Mo-roc - co, fetched as far as from Mo - roc - co, fetched as far as

- co, fetched as far as from Mo-roc - co, fetched as far, fetched as far as

- co, fetched as far as from Mo - roc - co, fetched as far as

- co, fetched as far as from Mo - roc - co, fetched as far as

from Mo - roc - co: Thy search-ing fume Ex-hales the_____ rheum,

from Mo - roc - co: Thy search-ing fume Ex - hales the rheum, ex - hales the rheum, thy

from Mo - roc - co: Thy search-ing fume Ex-

from Mo - roc - co: Thy search - ing fume, thy

from Mo - roc - co:

*C (transposed) in the original.

thy search-ing fume ex-

search - ing fume ex - hales the rheum, ex - hales the rheum, thy

- hales the rheum, ex - hales the rheum, ex - hales the_____ rheum,

search-ing fume Ex-hales the_____ rheum, ex - hales the rheum,

Thy search-ing fume ex - hales_____ the rheum,

- hales the rheum, thy search-ing fume ex hales the rheum, thy

search-ing fume ex-hales the rheum, thy search-ing fume ex-hales_ the rheum, thy search-ing fume ex-

thy search-ing fume ex-hales the_____ rheum, ex - hales the rheum,

thy search-ing fume ex-hales the rheum, ex - hales the rheum, thy

thy search-ing fume ex-hales the rheum, ex - hales the rheum,

2. COME, SIRRAH JACK, HO!

Thomas Weelkes (1576–1623)

1. Come, sir-rah Jack, ho! Fill some to-bac-co, Bring a wire And some
2. Fill the pipe once more, My brains dance Trench-more:† It is head-y, I am

1. Come, sir-rah Jack, ho! Fill some to-bac-co, Bring a wire And some
2. Fill the pipe once more, My brains dance Trench-more: It is head-y, I am

1. Come, sir-rah Jack, ho! Fill some to-bac-co, Bring a wire And some
2. Fill the pipe once more, My brains dance Trench-more: It is head-y, I am

Allegro ♩.= c. 60

mf repeat *p*

* B♭ has been omitted from key signature because B♮ (F♯ in original) predominates.
+Trenchmore: a lively country dance.

6

gear Than is here, By the rood, For the blood It is ve - ry, ve - ry good, 'tis ve - ry good. I good.
go Pluck a crow, And not know As I do The_ sweet of Tri - ni - da - do, Tri - ni - da - do. Then - da - do.

gear Than is here, By the rood, For the blood It is ve - ry, ve - ry good, 'tis ve - ry good. I good.
go Pluck a crow, And not know As I do The_ sweet of Tri - ni - da - do, Tri - ni - da - do. Then - da - do.

Bet - ter gear Than is here: For the blood 'Tis ve - ry good. I good.
Pluck a crow, And not know, For know the sweet of Tri - ni - da - do. Then - da - do.

last time **rall.**

3. TOBACCO FUMES AWAY

Thomas Ravenscroft (c. 1582 - c. 1635)

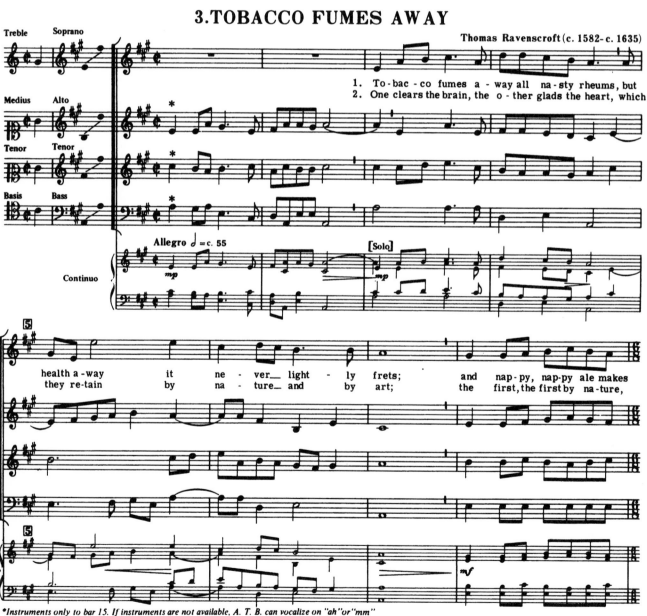

Treble Soprano

1. To - bac - co fumes a - way all na - sty rheums, but
2. One clears the brain, the o - ther glads the heart, which

Medius Alto

Tenor Tenor

Basis Bass

Allegro ♩ = c. 55

Continuo

health a - way it ne - ver_ light - ly frets; and nap - py, nap - py ale makes
they re - tain by na - ture_ and by art; the first, the first by na - ture,

*Instruments only to bar 15. If instruments are not available, A. T. B. can vocalize on "ah" or "mm"

8

+Crotchets: whimsical fancies.

* D in the original.

4. AHEY FOR AND AHO

John Wilson (1595 - 1674)

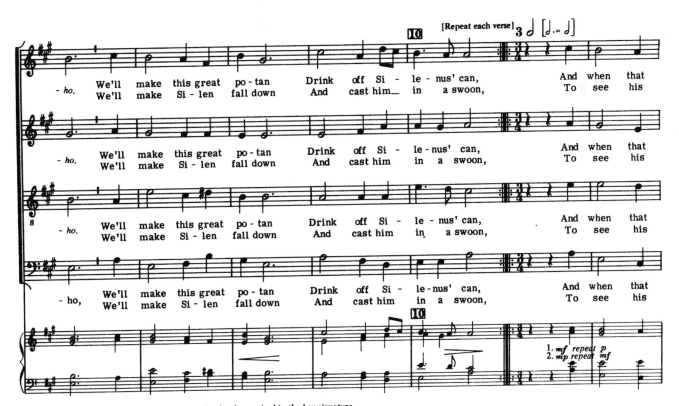

* G (F in original) is consistently sharpened and so has been raised in the key signature.
** "For and" = "and moreover". Possibly the same meaning is intended in no. 14.
+ Soprano is changed with Tenor from beginning to 1iii, 62iv - 63iii, and with Alto, 1iv - 2iii.
  63iv - 64iii, whose part is there given to Tenor. Alto and Tenor are interchanged 31ii - 32.

10

[Repeat each verse]

Silenus' side second time

3. Ka - wash - a comes in ma - je - sty, Was ne - ver such a god as he:

I° Tempo ♩ = c. 88

Choir 1
mf repeat *f*

* Pronounced "i-er" and "fi-er".

Up with singers, down with robbers. Don't photocopy.

*Verses 4 and 5 interpolated. See Editor's Notes.

5. GOOD, GOOD INDEED!

A Catch on Tobacco, to be sung by four men at the time of smoking their pipes

Henry Aldrich (1647-1710)

6. QUAND JE BOIS
(TOURDION)

Soprano. When I drink claret everything spins round; and it will be just the same when I drink wines of Anjou and Arbois. Let's sing and drink, and attack this flagon.
Alto. Good wine has cheered us up. Let's sing and forget our troubles. While we're eating this juicy ham, let's attack this flagon.
Tenor. Let's drink up; drink then and attack the flagon. While we're eating.....
Bass. Drink up, my friends, let's see the bottom of the glass. While we're eating.....

Anon, Attaignant, 1530

chan - tons et bu - vons, mes a - mis, bu - vons donc!

ce fla - con fai - sons la guer - re.

ce fla - con fai - sons la guer - re.

ce fla - con fai - sons la guer - re.

7. SO TRINKEN WIR ALLE

Let's all drink up this wine with gusto, for it is a prince among wines. Drink, my dear little Dieter, so you'll never be thirsty. Drink up, then!

Arnold von Bruck (c. 1490-1554)

So trin - ken wir al - le die - sen Wein

So trin - ken wir al - le die - sen Wein mit Schal - le!

So trin - ken wir al - le die - sen Wein mit Schal - le, mit Schal -

So trin - ken wir al - le die - sen

So trin - ken wir al - le die - sen Wein mit Schal - le! Die - ser

Andante con moto ♩ = c. 70

8. C'EST TROP PARLÉ DE BACCHUS

There's too much fuss over Bacchus and his drinking cup. That's old hat. Let's drink without pulling a face. Rouse yourselves, comrades, and let's all get together to drain tankards, flagons, pitchers and mugs. Without complaining, drink your fill continually, both morning and evening. I drink to you. Well then, make the most of it. Look at me without sighing over it: do I make a fuss?

Pierre Certon (c. 1510–1572)

22

9 . BACCO, BACCO

Bacchus, Bacchus e, u, o, e.

Francesco Corteccia (1502-71)

10. HOY COMAMOS Y BEBAMOS

1. Let's eat and drink, today, sing and be merry, for tomorrow we fast.
2. In honour of St. Carnival, let us glut ourselves today, fill our bellies and stuff our hides.
3. For it is an established tradition that we should all gorge ourselves today, for tomorrow we fast.
4. Let's honour such a good saint, because he will help us when we're hungry. Let's cram ourselves to the gills, for tomorrow there'll be a great scarcity.
5. Let's eat and drink till we burst, for tomorrow we fast.

Juan del Encina (1468– c. 1530)

24

6, 7. Bebe, Bras; más tú, Beneito
  Beba Pidruelo y Llorente;
  Bebe tú primeramente,
  Quitarnos has deste pleito.
  En beber bien me deleito
  Daca, daca, beberemos,
  Que mañana ayunaremos.

8, 9. Tomemos hoy gasalhado,
  Que mañana viene la muerte;
  Bebamos, comamos huerte;
  Vámonos para el ganado.
  No perderemos bocado,
  Que comiendo nos iremos,
  Que mañana ayunaremos.

6, 7. Drink up, Bras, and you Beneito;
  Let Pidruelo and Llorente drink.
  And you must drink first of all
  To break the deadlock.
  I take great delight in drinking:
  Come on, now, let's drink,
  For tomorrow we fast.

8, 9. Let's enjoy ourselves today,
  For tomorrow death comes.
  We must do some hard eating and drinking,
  Let's go join the herd.
  We wont miss a mouthful,
  But eat as we go,
  For tomorrow we fast.

11. TRINK ICH WEIN

1. If I drink wine I'll be ruined; if I drink water I'll die. Nevertheless, it's better to drink wine and be ruined than water and die. 2. Drinking wine brings ruin: you lose your possessions and you eventually have to pay the vintner: that's how it is on earth. 3. Drinking water causes illness and untimely weakness; a wise man should refrain from drinking it if he wants to live a long time. 4. (Yet, both,) water and the gift of the grape are good for medicinal purposes. They keep you healthy and are thus of considerable benefit.

Henning Dedekind (1562–1626)

3. Wasser trinken bringt Krankheit
   Und ungelegne Schwachheit.
   Wasser trinken hüte sich ein Weiser eben,
   So er will lange leben.

4. Wasser und Rebensgaben
   Gut Arzeneie haben,
   Dein Gesundheit können sie dir wohl beschützen,
   So du sie recht wirst nützen.

12. CANTO, CANTO, FESTA, FESTA

Singing and feasting dispel all sad spirits. Only pleasure and delight fill our breasts. Let's live forever

happy and always sing the praises of Bacchus.

Andrea Gabrieli (c. 1520–1586)

*Chorus of little children.

Bac - cho, Bac - ch'o - gn'hor can - tia - mo, Bac - cho, Bac - ch'o - gn'hor can - tia - mo.

Bac-cho, Bac - ch'o - gn'hor can - tia - mo, Bac-cho, Bac - ch'o - gn'hor can - tia - mo.

Bac - cho, Bac - ch'o - gn'hor can - tia - mo, Bac - cho, Bac - ch'o - gn'hor can - tia - mo.

Bac - cho, Bac - ch'o - gn'hor can - tia - mo, Bac - cho, Bac - ch'o - gn'hor can - tia - mo.

13. EIN GUTER WEIN

1. A good wine is to be praised above all other things on this earth, and I cannot forego it;
   whoever comes last to the drinking when the table is full must suffer in silence.
2. A large bumper of cool wine is a great joy to me, and it's now going the rounds:
   whoever wants to drink as much as I will also be made happy by this wine.

Orlandus Lassus (1532-94)

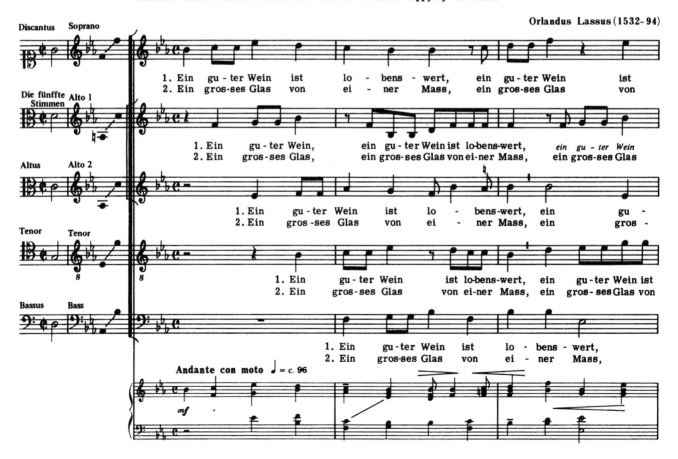

3. Mit einem Trunck in einem Funck
du ich dir nun das gar bringen.
Trincks auss' es wird dir' glingen!
Tusdu nit bschaid es ist mir laid,
ich derff dir gar Reins mer bringen,
Du solt auch nit mit singen.

*3. I'll bring you a drink in a flash. Drink up,
you're quite capable. Do it with conviction
and I'll be glad to bring you even more of
the same pure stuff, and then you must sing
with me.*

14. AVE COLOR VINI

All hail to thee, colour of clear wine; hail, taste without parallel. By your power you are worthy of inebriating us. O how happy is the person guided by the pure vine. May every table be made easy by your presence. How pleasing in hue, how fragrant a bouquet, how titillating to the palate, what a sweet slur to the tongue. How happy is the belly which you enter; happy the gullet that you numb; happy the mouth that you cause to stutter; O blessed lips! Therefore, let us all praise wine; let us exalt topers. Let us drinkers never be brought to confusion for ever and ever. Amen.

Juan Ponce (c. 1480-c. 1530)

32

+ G (transposed) in the original.

*Tenor and Bass switched 26i-ii.

...Lost sales lead to
shorter print runs...

*Semibreve without rest in the original.

34

15. GIVE US ONCE A DRINK

Thomas Ravenscroft (c. 1582 - c. 1635)

* Select an appropriate topic for each verse. At bar 9 the topics are declaimed accumulatively in reverse order, as are the liquid measures, bar 19ff., in a manner similar to "Green grow the rushes O." ** The Verses may be sung tutti and can move from part to part.
+ "For and" possibly means "and moreover". The present interpertation seems likelier.
++ Probably a corruption of "va à moi".

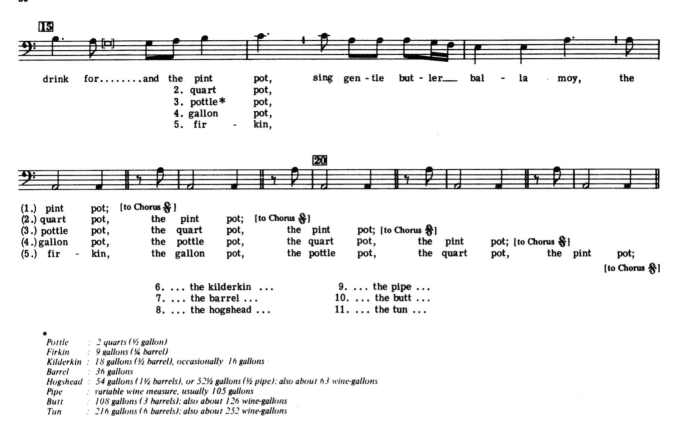

drink for........and the pint pot, sing gen - tle but - ler bal - la moy, the

2. quart pot,
3. pottle* pot,
4. gallon pot,
5. fir - kin,

(1.) pint pot; [to Chorus 𝄋]
(2.) quart pot, the pint pot; [to Chorus 𝄋]
(3.) pottle pot, the quart pot, the pint pot; [to Chorus 𝄋]
(4.) gallon pot, the pottle pot, the quart pot, the pint pot; [to Chorus 𝄋]
(5.) fir - kin, the gallon pot, the pottle pot, the quart pot, the pint pot;
[to Chorus 𝄋]

6. ... the kilderkin ...   9. ... the pipe ...
7. ... the barrel ...   10. ... the butt ...
8. ... the hogshead ...   11. ... the tun ...

*
Pottle : *2 quarts (½ gallon)*
Firkin : *9 gallons (¼ barrel)*
Kilderkin : *18 gallons (½ barrel), occasionally 16 gallons*
Barrel : *36 gallons*
Hogshead : *54 gallons (1½ barrels), or 52½ gallons (½ pipe); also about 63 wine-gallons*
Pipe : *variable wine measure, usually 105 gallons*
Butt : *108 gallons (3 barrels); also about 126 wine-gallons*
Tun : *216 gallons (6 barrels); also about 252 wine-gallons*

16. TOSS THE POT

Thomas Ravenscroft (c. 1582- c. 1635)

Toss the pot, toss the pot: let us be mer - ry, And drink till our cheeks be as

Verse

1. We take no thought, we have no care,
2. We drink, carouse with heart most free:
3. And when our money is all spent,

red as a cherry.

* Instruments only. If instruments are not available, A.T.B. can vocalize on "ah" or "mm", or sing the actual words of the top line.

For still we spend and never spare; Till of all money our
A hearty draught I drink to thee; Then fill the pot a-
Then sell our goods and spend our rent, Or drink it up with

purse is bare, we ever toss the pot.
-gain to me, and ever toss the pot.
one consent, and ever toss the pot.

4. When all is gone, we have no more:
    Then let us set it on the score,
    Or chalk it up behind the door,
        and ever toss the pot.
    Chorus: *Toss the pot ...*

5. And when our credit is all lost,
    Then we may go and kiss the post,
    And eat brown bread instead of roast,
        and ever toss the pot.
    Chorus: *Toss the pot ...*

6. Let us conclude as we began,
    And toss the pot from man to man,
    And drink as much now as we can,
        and ever toss the pot.
    Chorus: *Toss the pot ...*

...and more fine works are lost from the repertoire.

17. TRUDGE AWAY QUICKLY

Thomas Ravenscroft (c. 1582- c. 1635)

*D in the original.

*Instruments only. If instruments are not available, A.T.B. can vocalize on "ah" or "mm", or sing the actual words of the top line.

4. Master Butler, give us a taste
　　of your best drink so gently:
　A jug or twain, and make no waste,
　　for still methinks one tooth is dry.
　　　Chorus: *Trudge away.....*

5. Master Butler, of this take part:
　　ye love good drink as well as I:
　And drink to me with all your heart,
　　for still methinks one tooth is dry.
　　　Chorus: *Trudge away.....*

18. ROUNDS FROM RAVENSCROFT'S *PAMMELIA*

(i) BANBURY ALE

(ii) DONNEZ A BOIRE

Go and get me something to drink,
my good friend, alleluia.

Ban - bu - ry ale!

Where, where, where?

At the black-smith's house: I

would I were there!

*Don - nez à boire

al - lez, bon com - pa - ni -

- on, al - le-lu - ia,

al - le - lu - ia.

Original reads: "Donec aboire alle...."

(iii) NOW KISS THE CUP, COUSIN

Now kiss the cup, Cou-sin, with cour - te - sy,

And drink your part with a heart will - ing - ly:

Then so shall we all a-gree mer - ri - ly.

(iv) HE THAT WILL AN ALEHOUSE KEEP

He that will an ale-house keep must have three things in store: a

cham-ber and a fea-ther bed, a chim-ney and a hey non-ny non-ny,

hey non-ny non-ny, hey non-ny no, hey non-ny no, hey non-ny no.

(v) HEY DOWN A DOWN

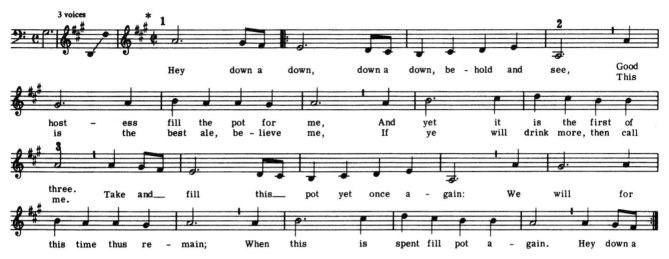

Hey down a down, down a down, be-hold and see, Good

host — ess fill the pot for me, And yet it is the first of
This is the best ale, be-lieve me, If ye will drink more, then call

three. Take and fill this pot yet once a-gain: We will for
me. Take and fill this pot yet once a-gain: We will for

this time thus re — main; When this is spent fill pot a-gain. Hey down a

* G (F in original) is consistently sharpened and so has been raised in the key signature.

(vi) HEY HO, NOBODOY AT HOME

(vii) WHITE WINE AND SUGAR

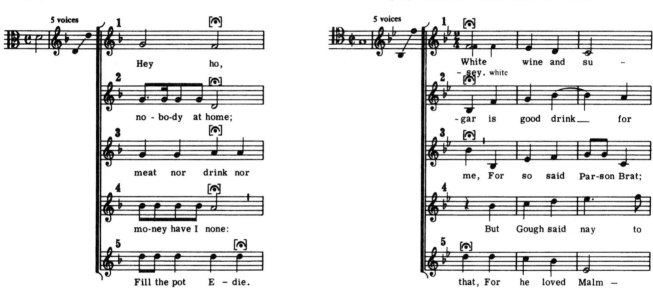

Hey ho,

White wine and su —

no-bo-dy at home;

-gar. white

meat nor drink nor

-gar is good drink for

mo-ney have I none:

me, For so said Par-son Brat;

Fill the pot E — die.

But Gough said nay to

that, For he loved Malm —

19. ROUNDS FROM *CATCH THAT CATCH CAN*

John Hilton (1599-1657)

(i) CALL GEORGE AGAIN, BOY

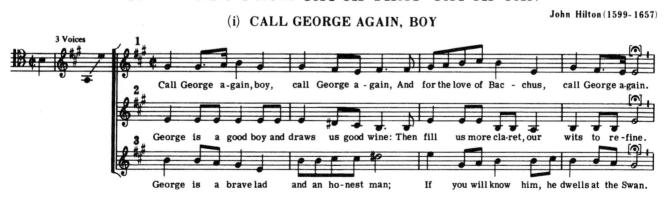

Call George a-gain, boy, call George a-gain, And for the love of Bac-chus, call George a-gain.

George is a good boy and draws us good wine: Then fill us more cla-ret, our wits to re-fine.

George is a brave lad and an ho-nest man; If you will know him, he dwells at the Swan.

(ii) IF YOU WILL DRINK FOR PLEASURE

(iii) O ALE AB ALENDO

(iv) O YES, O YES

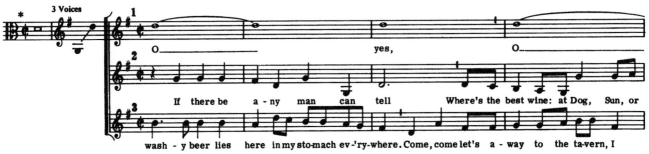

* *F♯ is consistently used in the original and so has been included in the key signature.*

EDITOR'S NOTES

1. General. This series is a thematic anthology of secular European madrigals and part-songs from the 16th and early 17th centuries. The settings are mainly for mixed four-part choir, but there are also some for three and five voices, and an occasional one for six. Five voices are strongly represented because this was an especially popular number in late 16th century madrigals. By and large, the items present relatively few vocal or harmonic difficulties for the fairly able choir, and where more than four parts are required, they are usually drawn from the upper voices (mainly the sopranos), with the tenor line hardly ever being split.

The term madrigal has been interpreted rather loosely. Besides the contrapuntal part-song, it relates to the frottola, ayre, chanson, lied and the villancico, whether courtly or folk (these all basically being harmonised melodies, often very simply set, and usually repeated for each stanza). More obviously, it encompasses the ballet (a short stanzaic setting in two sections with repeats and fa la las), and the canzonet (a lighter style madrigal, normally for a small number of voices). Rounds and catches have also been included because they were obviously an important component of a sing-song or a drinking party, certainly in 17th century England, and their choice of subject matter is very free-ranging. To help make madrigal concerts rather more of a party than a performance, at least two or three of the rounds in each volume have been selected as simple enough to be sung by an audience with or without a visual aid (see section 5 of these notes).

One of the most important features of this anthology is the arrangement by subjects, each volume being devoted to one of the prevalent topics in secular songs, for example, "The Animal Kingdom" (vol. 1), "Love and Marriage" (vol. 2) and "Desirable Women" (vol. 3). This provides not only a new approach to madrigal anthologies but also, more importantly, a focus for the singers and, it is hoped, a comprehensible, appetising programme for the audience. Thus, it should be possible to provide a short concert entirely from one of these volumes, and two halves of a longer concert from any two.

Each volume contains at least twelve part-songs and, on average, half a dozen rounds. About one-third of the texts are in English, but an attempt has been made to provide a representative collection of Italian and French lyrics, and, to a lesser extent, of German and Spanish. The selection combines indispensable popular works with a fair mixture of relatively unfamiliar but attractive and singable pieces. Some thought has also been given to affording a balance between the lively and the reflective, the happy and the sad, for the sake of variety of mood and to help mirror the ups and downs of Renaissance life, though in this volume the downs usually come the morning after.

2. Editorial method. As with the Chester Latin Motet series, the Editor has endeavoured to make the volumes suitable for both performance and study. The madrigals are transposed, where necessary, into the most practical keys for ease of vocal range, are barred, fully underlaid in modernised spelling and punctuation, are provided with breathing marks, and have a simplified reduction as a rehearsal aid or as a basis for a continuo. Editorial tempi and dynamics have been supplied, but only in the reduction, leaving conductors free to supply their own according to their interpretation, vocal resources and the acoustics. The vocal range is given at the beginning of each piece, as also are translations for the non-English texts.

To help musicologists, the madrigals are transcribed from the most authoritative sources available. Original clefs, signatures and note values are given at the beginning and wherever they change during the course of a piece. Ligatures are indicated by slurs, editorial accidentals are placed above the stave, and the underlay is shown in italics when it expands a ditto sign, or in square brackets if entirely editorial. When the original contains a *basso continuo*, it is included as the bass line of the reduction. Finally, each volume contains brief notes on the scope of the edition, the composers, stylistic features of the part-songs, and the sources used, while editorial emendations and changes are given in footnotes in the text proper.

3. The tobacco songs. Smoking is recorded as early as the 5th century, B.C., when Herodotus writes of a Scythian tribe which made itself high on fumes from a fire apparently made with Indian hemp. Tobacco, long cultivated by the Indians of North and South America mainly for ritual and medicinal purposes, was first noted by Europeans in November 1492, when two sailors sent by Columbus to explore Cuba found natives puffing smoke from their mouths and noses. Some forty years later, Jacques Cartier encountered Indians on the banks of the St. Lawrence sucking powdered leaves through hollowed pieces of wood or stone. Though neither Columbus nor Cartier utilised this discovery, tobacco nevertheless found its way to Europe by the mid-16th century. In 1556, or thereabouts, the French ambassador to Portugal, Jean Nicot (from whom Nicotine derives its name), purchased some tobacco seed from a Flemish merchant newly arrived from Florida and sent it to the Grand Prior of France; he also presented a few tobacco plants to Catherine de Medici on his return to France in 1561, recommending it, with curious success, as a medicine. Around 1559, a Spanish physician, Francesco Hernandez, brought back some plants from Mexico for inspection by Philip II of Spain. The Spaniards, Hernandez among them, called the plant *tobaco*, the Indian word which (as Orviedo had observed in *Historia de las Indias*, 1526) was the name for the forked pipe through which the Indians inhaled tobacco smoke into the nostrils, though it also applied to the rolled leaf prepared for smoking. The name prevailed, despite being rivalled for a time by several others, including, in France, *Herbe du Grand Prieur, Herbe de la Reine, Herbe Medicée*, and *Nicotiane;* and in Italy, *Erba Santa Croce* and *Tornabona* - after a cardinal and an envoy respectively who first introduced the plant there.

Tobacco seems to have been first imported into England from Florida by Sir John Hawkins in 1565, and then possibly by Sir Francis Drake from the West Indies in 1573. Another early importer was the governor of Virginia, Ralph Lane (1586), who is also thought to have been the first notable Elizabethan to smoke it in public. Whereas on the Continent tobacco was used mainly as a medicine - often being taken, as in France, in the form of snuff - the English quickly became addicted to smoking it (or "drinking" it in Renaissance terminology), not only for health but also for sheer enjoyment. The fashion spread quickly: in 1576, Lobelius noted in *Novum Stirpium Adversaria*, that within a few years tobacco had become an inmate of England, chiefly from the influence of the sailors returning from America carrying little funnels of palm leaves or reeds with rolled or powdered tobacco stuffed in one end ready for smoking. Harrison's *Description of England* (1587) likewise notes that by 1573, there was a very common practice of "taking-in smoke of the Indian herbe called Tobaco, by an instrument formed like a little ladell". Sir Walter Ralegh, though he must be denied his traditional place as the introducer of tobacco in England, nevertheless helped to make smoking fashionable at court, and is said to have tricked Queen Elizabeth into tolerating the habit by wagering with her that he could weigh tobacco smoke, winning his bet by simply causing his pipe to be weighed before and after he smoked it and subtracting the difference.

English smokers (who included a handful of daring women) generally used a long-stemmed clay pipe for the "drinking", but metal ones, especially of silver, were also employed. The habit was extremely expensive: in the late 16th century, Sir Henry Sidney paid three shillings an ounce for his tobacco, and even by the early 17th century it was around eighteen shillings a pound – as compared, for example, with a quart of ale costing a penny.

Tobacco is hailed in verse and song and celebrated in plays. Spenser praises its curative properties in the *Fairy Queen* and Jonson features it in *The Alchemist, Bartholomew Fair*, and several other plays. Not all were convinced of its beneficial effect, however, and many, including the Puritans, condemned it as a pernicious vice. One of the leading opponents was James I, who in his *Counterblaste to Tobacco* (1603) concentrates on its anti-social aspects and its gruesome effect on the stomach and lungs. In time, most rulers in Europe and beyond reacted against tobacco and introduced strict controls, often in the form of a monopoly, though its popularity continued to grow, with the convenient and relatively inexpensive cigarette eventually becoming the dominant form for consumption.

Songs about tobacco are rare on the Continent until the later 17th century, and although they are quick to appear in England, are still not that numerous until the Restoration. The five items on tobacco in this anthology are fulsome in their praise of its medicinal and convivial effects. The first of these, *O metaphysical tobacco*, seems to be the earliest madrigal on the subject, deriving from Michael East's *Second Set of Madrigales ... Apt for Viols and Voices,* 1606 (copy in British Library). The composer, in all likelihood the son of the music printer, Thomas East, was born around 1580. Little is known of him except that he was in the service of the Lord Chancellor, Sir Christopher Hatton, for a time, and later became choirmaster of Lichfield Cathedral. His works include an evening service, anthems, and six books of madrigals. The short lyric for the present madrigal apostrophises tobacco as "metaphysical" (i.e. transcendent), mainly because it clears the head of rheum (catarrh). Oddly enough, this brand has been brought from "Morocco" – a convenient near-rhyme for tobacco – rather than directly from the Americas. East may have compiled this untaxing lyric himself; he certainly dressed it in a lively imaginative setting in circular form (aba), with an effective mixture of homophony for the opening and closing invocation and a frisky pair of fugues adorned with word-painting for the middle section.

Thomas Weelkes (biographical details in Volume 1) can often be relied on for unusual texts, and *Come, Sirrah Jack, ho* provides no exception. It derives from his *Ayres or Phantasticke Spirites for Three Voices,* 1608 (copy in British Library), as does the musically similar *Strike it up, tabor* (Volume 5). The preference here is for Trinidadian tobacco, which evokes an almost phrenetic desire to "drink it" with the aid of a wire pipe-cleaner, a newly-filled pipe and "some fire". The claims made for tobacco are much more ambitious than in the previous song: the speaker, with an un-Protestant gesture, swears by the cross and the mass that it will purify the blood and purge the body of all its aches and pains – including those in the back and kidneys ("reins"). The setting has two short repeated sections, the first in triple time and the second in duple. It makes extended use of descending sequences in both sections, in the first of which the bass sings in consecutive tenths with the soprano, while the highly syncopated alto (bar 4ff.) enters fractionally later in a canon at the fourth.

One of the great popularisers of songs at the beginning of the 17th century was Thomas Ravenscroft (biographical details in Volume 1). He includes tobacco as one of the pleasures to be extolled in his *Briefe Discourse*, 1614 (copy in British Library), where it keeps company with hunting, hawking, dancing, drinking and "enamouring". In a type of "witty conceit", *Tobacco fumes away* delineates the virtues and shortcomings of the two jovial companions, smoking and drinking. The superior, tobacco, clears the head of catarrh and the brain of vapours; nappy (i.e. strong, heady) ale warms the heart but quickly befuddles the brain. The combination of the two is likely to turn us into giddy fools, causing our brains to swell with "crotchet rules" (fantastic ideas) – an effect similar to "taking a trip". Ravenscroft uses a solo voice and three instruments for the verse and four-part chorus for the refrain, a technique common to most of his songs in *A Briefe Discourse*. As usual, the harmony is simple and serviceable — but the melody is varied and relatively complex - so is the rhythm, which encompasses two forms of duple time and one of triple, and includes much syncopation, together with a succession of swift figures as the frenzy swells in the brain.

Tobacco also finds a place in an antimasque song, *Ahey for and aho,* from the *Masque of Flowers*, 1614 (copy in British Library). The composer, John Wilson (1595-1674), perhaps best known for his Shakespeare songs, was also a lutenist and singer. He became a musician to Charles I and later Gentleman of the Chapel Royal in the reign of Charles II, having shortly before been professor of music at Oxford, where he had obtained a doctorate in music in 1645. *Ahey for and aho* constitutes a debate between, on the one hand, the followers of Silenus, the traditional acolyte of Bacchus, depicted here as an old fat man with swollen red face, bottle nose, bald pate, prick ears and little horns, and, on the other, the adherents of the tobacco chief, Kawasha, an Indian complete with bows and arrows, clad in tobacco leaves and with a chimney for a crown. The stage directions indicate that the singers for Silenus are dressed as a miller, wine cooper, vintner's boy and brewer, being accompanied by tabor and pipe, treble and bass "violin", sackbut and mandora. For Kawasha, the singers are a shipper, fencer, pedlar and barber, supported by "bass violin", tenor cornett and sackbut (see further, in E.A.J. Honigmann, *Book of Masques*). The text of the antimasque includes several verses not found in the setting (among them verses 4 and 5, set editorially here), though they were clearly performed, being "frumpled over" by the "fiddlers". This lively, bustling and unpretentious strophic song is set mainly in simple harmonic and monosyllabic style, the emphasis being clearly on the words. Unless performances of this piece are to be "dressed up" according to the full stage directions, it is probably better to ignore all the repeats.

The last paean of praise for tobacco in this volume is a 4-part round, *Good, good indeed*, first published in *The Second Book of the Pleasant Musical Companion*, 1687 (copy in British Library). It was written by that renowned smoker, Dr. Henry Aldrich (1647-1710), who was also a composer, theologian and architect. A first-rate university administrator, he became dean of Christ Church Oxford in 1689, and vice chancellor in 1692. He was so addicted to tobacco that he was said to refrain from smoking only when he was filling his pipe, a notion borne out by the fact that *Good, good indeed* makes liberal provision for rests so that, as the sub-title of the round indicates, it can be sung by four men while smoking their pipes. (For further reading on tobacco in the period see Jerome E. Brooks, *Tobacco: Its History Illustrated*, 4 vols., 1937-43, and F.W. Fairholt, *Tobacco: Its History and Associations,* 1859, reissued 1968).

4. The drinking songs. Drinking has always been a popular pleasure and source of conviviality, and despite all the warnings and attacks of moralists, it was clearly as common a pastime in the Renaissance as in any previous or subsequent age. Drinking songs of the period exist in great abundance, though to judge from the madrigals this would not appear to be the case, especially since their lyrics are generally on an idealised plane. Songs celebrating drink seem to have been generally the property of the middle and lower orders of society and are usually relatively unsophisticated. It is noticeable too that they are more common in Northern Europe than in the Mediterranean countries, being especially prevalent in Germany. These two points are alluded to by Thomas Morley in the third part of his *Plain and Easy Introduction to Practical Music*:

> The slightest kind of music (if they deserve the name of music) are the *vinate,* or drinking songs ... but that vice [of drinking] being so rare among the Italians and Spaniards, I rather think that music to have been devised by or for the Germans (who in swarms do flock to the University of Italy) rather than for the Italians themselves.

Broadly speaking, the songs that come from the Mediterranean countries are mainly concerned with wines, whereas the Northern traditions are understandably more in favour of ale or beer; though some German song collections, for example those of Georg Forster, incline very much to the grape.

The honour of the first drinking song in this collection has, however, to go to France (a devotee of its own wines but not overly given to singing about them), with the famous but anonymous *Tourdion* published by Attaignant in *Neuf Bases Dances*, f.iii, 1530 (copy in Bayerishche Staatsbibliothek, Munich). The tourdion, a lively dance in triple time, has no lyrics attached: these were added later. In one of the most tuneful melodies ever devised, the frisky soprano line describes the effect of "vin clairet" and the produce of Anjou and Arbois; while the underpinning lower lines give a call to arms to attack the flagon and a side of ham.

A similarly popular German piece is *So trinken wir alle*, item 30 in Georg Forster's *Der Ander Theil*, 1540 (copy in Bayerische Staatsbibliothek, Munich). The composer, Arnold von Bruck (c. 1490-1554) was an Austrian of Flemish origin. Although Kapellmeister to the Emperor Ferdinand I for about twenty years, he seems to have had Lutheran leanings, as appears from the many chorales he wrote. He composed mainly for the vernacular, and his secular songs were very highly regarded and anthologised. *So trinken wir alle* is in some ways like a piece of ebullient but sophisticated polyphony. The tenor constitutes the *cantus firmus*, presumably based on the original drinking song (which had three verses), and this is freely imitated by the other parts, in particular, the first soprano. Swaying jocularity is suggested by the vigorous duple time, and the final repeated phrases suitably convey a compelling insistence for all to drink up.

Pierre Certon (c. 1510-72) spent most of his life in Paris and was master of the boys' choir of Sainte Chapelle for thirty years. He composed a great deal of sacred and secular vocal music, being especially celebrated for his *chansons polyphoniques*, of which *C'est trop parlé de Bacchus* is a good example. Like many of Certon's chansons, it was published by Attaignant, appearing as item 15 of *Vingt et six chansons,* 1535 (copy in Bayerische Staatsbibliothek, Munich). Similar in form to the madrigal, the chanson moves at great pace in a series of short fugues, with only a slight overlap. The music keeps a clear eye on the shape and meaning of the words in a manner reminiscent of both Jannequin and Passereau, though Certon's style is nevertheless fairly distinctive. Above all, the musical texture ably conveys the buoyant and defiant spirit of its text, and sustains momentum to the end.

The composer of *Bacco, Bacco*, Francesco Corteccia (1502-1571), was a Florentine who held the coveted post of director of music to Cosimo de' Medici, providing (in collaboration) the music for many court festivities, the first being for Cosimo's wedding. *Bacco, Bacco* forms part of that entertainment, being the epilogue to Antonio Landi's comedy, *Il Comodo*, for which Corteccia provided the interludes. It was published, along with all the music for that notable entertainment, in *Musiche fatti nella nozze dello illustrissimo Duca di Fierenze*, 1539 (complete set of copies in the Österreichische Nationalbibliothek, Vienna). The stage directions, somewhat in anticipation of the *Masque of Flowers* mentioned above, specify twenty bacchantes for musicians, eight of them playing varying instruments, eight singing, and two on each side pretending to be drunk. The dancers comprised four satyrs and four ladies, all carrying small lighted torches in the right hand, and in the left, drinking vessels, a tambourine or raw meat. The music was repeated incessantly, accompanied by loud, drunken laughter. The sprightly nonsense song with its catchy fragment of tune was obviously a perfect vehicle for such a performance (see further, A. C. Minor and B. Mitchell, *A Renaissance Entertainment*, 1968).

Juan del Encina (biographical details in Volume 2) is a master of short, lively villancicos, and provides a little masterpiece of melody and rhythm to celebrate drinking and eating in carnival time: *Hoy comamos y bebamos*, transcribed here from Cancionero Musical de Palacio manuscript, MS. 1335, ff. 105v.-106, Palacio Real, Madrid. The setting lends itself to accompaniment and solos, which can be drawn from either the soprano or tenor line. An equally brief strophic setting, though far more transparent and simple, is provided by Henning Dedekind (1562-1626), a German composer and music theorist from Lower Saxony, whose main vocation was theology and preaching. From 1585, Dedekind was first Kantor at Langensalza, then a deacon and morning preacher at St. Bonifazius. In 1615 he was pastor at Gebesee, holding the position till his death. Few of Dedekind's works are extant, and most of them are to be found in the three-part song collection, *Dodekatonon Musicum Tricinorum*, 1588 (copy in Bayerische Staatsbibliothek, Munich), from which *Trink ich wein* is taken. The whimsical text (which should be sung *in toto*) is heavily based on syllogism and paradox, both of which are well served by this clear-cut, well punctuated, monosyllabic setting.

The great Venetian composer, Andrea Gabrieli is remarkable for the range of his sacred and secular music. He was capable of producing complex polychoral music suitable for St. Mark's (where he became first organist in 1584) and quite simple works, like the *Missa Brevis* or, in this case, *Canta, canta*, which derives from his *Madrigali et ricercari ... a quattro voci* (complete set of copies in the Bibliothèque Royale Albert Premier). Like Corteccia's *Bacco, bacco*, to which it has strong stylistic similarities, it was probably originally composed for a festival involving masque elements, since it was to be sung, and presumably danced, by a chorus of cupids or little boys.

Orlandus Lassus (biographical details in Volume 1) is much more versatile even than Gabrieli, and writes on every imaginable topic. For drinking songs, Lassus generally used German texts, and his settings of them, though rarely inspired, at least provide a stirring joviality. *Ein guter Wein* is a fairly early work, being published in *Neue teüsche Liedlein*, 1567 (complete set of copies in the Stadtbücherei, Heilbronn). It is remarkably restrained harmonically: the cadences are frequent and predictable, and the only modulation is into the related dominant. The style, however, is remarkably mixed after it's opening *stretto* fugue; there is a general "business", considerable fragmentation and frequent syncopation: all seemingly designed to simulate drunkeness – a notion reinforced by the many leaps and drops in the bass – while the overall sense of pace reflects the eagerness to join the drinking session.

Juan Ponce (c. 1480-1530), provides a good example of motet parody in this volume, a technique which seems to parallel the use of Marian epithets for describing the Petrarchan mistress. Relatively little is known of this Spanish composer. He seems to have been a member of a noble family from Aragon, and was a singer in the court of King Ferdinand, after whose death he may have entered the service of Charles V. Only one of his sacred compositions has survived and a dozen secular part-songs, all contained in the Cancionero Musical manuscript mentioned above. One of these, *Ave color vini,* was composed while Ponce was studying at the University of Salamanca, and is a setting of a student drinking-song, based on a late mediaeval goliardic text. The verse imitates hymns both to Christ and the Virgin, being a pastiche parodying such famous sacred texts as the *Ave verum, Crux fidelis, Lauda Sion* and *Ave Virgo, gratia plena*. The closest musical models for the parody seem to be the motets of Josquin des Près, as exemplified by *Ave Maria* (published in Volume 4 of the motet series). The similarities can be clearly seen in the frequent antiphonal pairings of high and low voices – often closing on the unison – the slow, measured pace, the homophonic texture, particularly in the tutti sections, and the change to triple time for moments of special devotion.

Understandably, Ravenscroft's publications are the source for the rest of the drinking songs. All three are based on lively and fairly unusual texts, and are couched in the form of solo verse and chorus refrain. *Give us once a drink* appears in *Deuteromelia,* 1609 (copy in British Library), in all likelihood harmonised by Ravenscroft himself. The original tune and words are probably not his, and it is as well to note that the lyric was first published in Marston's *Jack Drum's Entertainment,* 1601, as if it were currently very popular. The general style resembles that of a *Green grow the rushes* accumulative song, with unaccompanied solo voice leading off. Since there is ambiguity in "for and"(bars 2-4 and 8-10), in which "and" may simply intensify the force of "for", but could have a conjunctive reference to an implied substantive to match the catalogue of liquid measures, the Editor has taken the liberty of supplying two extra bars (3 and 9) to provide an *ad libitum* sequence, though they can be easily ignored. *Toss the pot* and *Trudge away quickly* are very similar companion songs both in melody and rhythm. They appear together in Ravenscroft's *Briefe Discourse,* 1614, where they are both ascribed to him, and in the table of contents, *Trudge away quickly* (item 10) is entitled *Of beer*, and *Toss the pot* (item 11) *Of ale*. The two pieces exhibit a convincing *joie de vivre* and a euphoric sense of *perpetuum mobile.*

Drinking rounds are numerous in 17th century English song books. Ravenscroft's works are thickly clustered with them, all the present examples being found in *Pammelia,* 1609 (copy in British Library), except for *He that will an alehouse keep,* which was published in *Melismata,* 1611 (copies of both works in the British Library and in facsimile). They are all tuneful and fairly inventive, and at least one of them, *Hey ho, nobody at home* has a ring of modernity which has ensured it a continued popularity, even though both the words and the tune have been adapted over the centuries. The same abundance of material is to be found in John Hilton's *Catch That Catch Can,* 1651 (copy in British Library and in facsimile), in which the rounds are rather more extended than in Ravenscroft, and a little more ambitious.

5. Notes on Programming. Since suggestions for performance have been stated at length in previous volumes, they are merely summarized here.

(i). The madrigals can be supplemented with solo songs on the same theme.

(ii). Readings can be interspersed with the music.

(iii). A cyclorama or screen can be used to project slides of works of art which correspond to the music performed in theme, period and, where possible, nationality.

(iv). The audience should be encouraged to join in rounds and songs. The words and music can be projected on the screen or cyclorama used for the slides.